Jagged on the Inside

By Kiri

First published in Great Britain in 2021

This story is based on real life events. All names have been changed and / or assigned a letter at random in order to protect the identity and privacy of individuals.

Design, typesetting and publishing by UK Book Publishing

www.ukbookpublishing.com

ISBN: 978-1-914195-25-9

Contents

For my mother

"The thoughts of others
Were light and fleeting,
Of lovers' meeting
Or luck or fame.
Mine were of trouble,
And mine were steady,
So I was ready
When trouble came."
~ A.E. Housman

Part I. Oxford

"It dropped so low in my regard
I heard it hit the ground,
And go to pieces on the stones
At the bottom of my mind"
~ Disenchantment, Emily Dickinson

If you were to do a cross section of me across the waistline, separating my top half from my bottom half, you would see the rings of a tree. As you trace your eyes along it from the core through its radius and out to the circumference, you would see the rings get progressively smoother, as the years of my life progress. This is not a perfect formation; jagged rings return here and there where trauma strikes over and again. This is the story I will tell, not of the smooth, but of the rougher years of my life so far.

As I write this, I begin to wonder whether I am narcissistic, as well as depressive and anxious. Is my life so important that the world must hear about it? Why me, when there are countless others suffering more than myself? I who have had the privilege of a great education, from primary to secondary school, and onto studying at some of the finest universities in the world.

Just because I have studied neuroscience, I do not think I am the authority on the brain and on mental health, though admittedly, I would like to claim the latter one day. Rather, I am writing this book to lend my voice and my story to countless others who may have themselves, or witnessed those they love, suffer through mental health problems or endure trauma. I want to share my story so that it may in some way bring comfort to those who feel alone, to educate those who wish to learn more about the grave impact of mental health issues, and for myself, as to share my story is to lift a weight off my shoulders with which I have long been burdened.

~

Oxford is where my journey of self-discovery truly begins. The year is 2010. I arrive at Baron College for Michaelmas of my first year of undergraduate studies, where I shall matriculate, settle into my new ensuite room on the main quad, and nervously await freshers' week which shall shape not only my university experience, but come to define the next ten years of my life.

Indeed, what a privilege it is to have gained the opportunity to study here. Throughout my teenage years, I worked steadfastly to gain straight A*s and to follow in the footsteps of my half-sister to study at Oxford. I would later learn that these teenage years were where my depression and anxiety really rooted themselves, and that upon winning my university place, I would start to steadily decline into a most profound and near fatal state of being.

But looking back, there were clearly signs that I was unwell as a teenager. At the age of 13, after a childhood of being bombarded by images of perfectly thin and exceptionally beautiful actresses and models in the media, I felt an overwhelming sense to strive for physical perfection. I started to skip breakfast and eat nothing but a raisin scone, a banana and a small bread roll from the school canteen for lunch every day, leaving myself languid during school hours. Returning home from school, I would force myself to do a thousand bicycle crunches, twenty sit ups and ten minutes of running on the spot. I would then proceed to eat just a bowl of Amazing K (the magical thinning cereal) with skimmed milk and an apple, with a cup of tea, before forcing myself upstairs at 6pm every day to start a gruelling evening of homework in my bedroom, the room I still call my haven despite some haunting memories of my time there. I would hesitate to return downstairs for dinner with my grandparents, father, sister and two older brothers (when they were still at home), and when I did go down, I ate sparingly.

These habits of intense work and low caloric intake persisted over the weekends, and for many years well into my 20s. When I went to school, only one friend noticed that I was, in her words, "wasting away". This became clear not only from my gaunt features but also from the many times I fainted at school. I was sent to the nurse's office after these spells to recover for some hours, an experience which involved sitting alone in a dank grey room littered with unused sick bowls, thermometers and bandages, wondering if anyone was going to talk to me about what happened. No one did talk to me about it, and I was often sent back to class or even home without much further consideration. Indeed, no one apart from myself thought to investigate the cause of this fainting. Unsurprisingly, I found out from the doctors that I was anaemic. I was sent away with ferrous sulphate tablets to fix the physical symptoms, but again, no one really asked why. Why was I not eating? Worse still, missing lessons for these spells only added to my anxiety and made me want to work even harder than usual to catch up. I was punishing myself.

Such pressure to look perfect was not made any easier for me as I suffered from relentless and agonising eczema as a young child until I was about 20 years old, when it cleared up somewhat miraculously by itself (though it did unfortunately transform into asthma). It left behind scars and stretch marks that persist to this day. Being bullied for the scratches and marks on my face, arms and legs in an all-girls school – where many of the girls had not only beautiful skin but could apply makeup to enhance it which I could not for the irritation it would cause my broken skin – served to deeply dent my self-esteem. I remember reading Mary Shelley's *Frankenstein* and thinking, I am the creature. I am vile and disgusting, no one will think I am beautiful or attractive, and worse still, I am wretched and awful because of this. This for me was encapsulated in such lines as *"I was benevolent and good; misery made me a fiend. Make me happy, and I shall again be virtuous"*. As I will talk about later in this story, I also noticed an abnormal symmetry in the movements of my hands as I scratched at both legs and both sides of my arms and face. This strange twitching of movement in my hands made me feel even more abnormal, even more monstrous. I was a clever and kind girl, but I was also a freak.

It was not just intense pressure to look perfect, but to *be* perfect – perfectly kind, perfectly polite and most excruciatingly, perfectly intelligent. In the school environment, such perfect intelligence is measurable and demonstrable through gaining full marks on exams. I had to get to Oxford, I wanted to, and I thought my family would not have otherwise, and the only way I could get there was to get perfect marks on everything I ever did. So I laboured night and day to achieve this. I recall becoming so stressed in the days leading up to my exams, that I would actually sleep during the afternoons, and stay up all night before heading straight to an exam, lest all the knowledge should fall out of my head in sleep. This was perhaps one of my unhealthiest habits of all (I am thankful I did not drink alcohol till I was 19, nor have I taken recreational drugs).

These preposterous notions of perfection and habits of self-destruction in the form of poor eating and sleeping habits I would later learn were all symptomatic of intense anxiety and major depressive disorder (MDD), which were soon to take an unendurable hold on my mind. In some ways, I do not regret pressuring myself in the ways that I did (or feeling the pressures placed upon me externally) or for such steely determination. It did bring me the successes I longed for, and it has made me a more intelligent and thoughtful adult.

Yet, I know now that had I gone to any one of the adults in my vicinity growing up and asked them why I felt the way I did – stressed, low and constantly tired – not one of them would have guessed at a mood disorder. Indeed, none of them even knew or believed (or wanted to believe) such things existed, let alone how to intervene when faced with them. And my family – already struggling after the death of my mother in 1993 and the sickness of my grandparents and disabled uncle with whom we lived - certainly did not want to acknowledge anything was the matter with me. I was the golden child, the youngest, and I had opportunities none of them could even imagine. How could I be broken? I can't afford to be broken, not in this family. All that was mentioned of it was my siblings saying in passing to me every so often "you are so moody all the time". This is what I heard time and time again as a teenager, but nothing was done to help it. No one did anything. But how can I blame them if they simply did not know; even I did not really know until much later.

You may be wondering what this all has to do with Oxford. Let me return to Michaelmas of 2010. A "fresher" or "freshman" is defined as a "a first-year student at university". What the dictionary does not say is that a fresher is a first-year student at university, who because of their youth and naivety, is often ridiculed, forced to attend debauched parties and drink alcohol (if not worse) in order to make friends (and connections if you go to a university like I went to). If you are a young lady, older students feel it their right to ogle at you as if you were fresh meat on the market. Worse still if you are an ethnic lady, and by the seemingly smartest, get called "exotic" and asked all about your "Indian heritage".

Let me clarify by saying yes, I am Punjabi; but I was born in New York in the USA and have lived in London since I was 4 years old. I was not close to my extended family growing up and hardly speak Punjabi (despite my father's attempts to take me to Saturday school in Wembley as a child). Regardless of where I am from, the best and brightest took it upon themselves to notice and point out: the colour of my skin (and to sexualise this), the fact that I am Indian (often when it had nothing to do with the conversation we were having) and from that, to expect me to be able to answer every single question relating to Indian-ism or even Asia and Africa because of my heritage. The best and brightest can be terribly ignorant.

It was for me the single worst way in which to commence what I hoped to be a glittering academic experience at a place I thought of as pure, of elevated thinking and superior morality and respect. Perhaps I was naïve to believe wholeheartedly that Oxford cultivated the best and brightest and most noble of men and women who could change and shape the world for the better. The realisation from the outset that my ideal notion of the place was woefully wrong, that in reality it was tarnished and debased by a handful of – though highly intelligent – arrogant, egotistical and self-absorbed students who crossed my path, was a deep and incalculable disappointment for me. Worst of all, I was not warned about it and was therefore entirely unprepared.

I was even more unprepared for seeing these behaviours in some of the graduate students and teaching staff. My increasing disillusionment would ultimately derail me and lead me to fall sick before my first-year exams with major depression, fail one exam (though I would pass the re-take later in the summer and continue at Oxford), and to re-orient my entire sense of being. I was lucky in some ways to have been studying neuroscience as part of my natural sciences course, and to be in a position to diagnose myself before a doctor did, and to learn more about the condition from which I was suffering so acutely from at least one or two academics at the forefront. I know that others like me were not so fortunate.

I place my blame not only on my own naivety and my acceptance and absorption of the actions of these other students and academics, but also on the systemic lack of support offered by the university (which I know is not unique to Oxford). As I say, these are the best and brightest, and why was it – despite being in the medical department most of the time, surrounded by not only students, but scientists and doctors at the pinnacle of their profession – that not one person noticed I was suffering from depression? Further still, even if they did notice, why did no one do anything to help me until it was almost too late? This place is meant to be a symbol of greatness and academic rigour to the world, a beacon of hope for the future, and it could not even help me, one of its students, when I was at my worst and when this illness was staring directly at them. Where was the pastoral support, and why when I felt my weakest, did I have to actively go and seek help?

To my best and most trusted friends and advisors from the university – which are a select but extremely dear few to whom I am forever grateful – I have asked these questions. It is clear to us all that more needs to be done. Ultimately – though it is difficult for me to admit this – despite the prominence of the place, I cannot pretend that Oxford served me very well and I sometimes regret attending Baron College despite the advantages it has given me in my now working life. The trauma was too great for any soul to bear and I feel fortunate I made it through these turbulent years alive and relatively intact.

~

I have skirted over my exact experiences with others at the time because it pains me deeply to think, let alone write about it. But with earnest consideration of those I might help by telling these stories here, I am given strength and courage to tackle it. In a set of five stories about active betrayal and inadequate support, I present the experiences that during my university years, put me on the edge of life and made me question my very reason for living.

Case 1 | The case of V

I start again in freshers' week, where I met a variety of students both new and resident. Among those in the year above was a young man I shall refer to as V. We were immediately drawn to each because of our mutual heritage, it must be said. The colour of one's skin has a tendency to impact who talks to you first in such settings, even in this day and age.

V was petite, but had chiselled features, as well as a bad-boy confidence that provided an allure to the sweet, innocent, girl-next-door embodiment that I was at the time. We met at several events in this week, but it was not until the following week – Week 1 of Michaelmas – that he officially asked me out on a date. I am not shy to admit that I was a virgin at the time, of the purest kind. I was saving myself for the right person, the true gentleman who would treat me with the dignity, respect and if not love, certainly kindness and due consideration that all creatures deserve.

Whilst on the face of it, V seemed like a princely, though sometimes haughty, gentleman, this swiftly changed on the evening of our first date. It was hardly a date, more of a conversation as we walked to and from one of Oxford's many (dreadful) clubs and returned to sit on a bench on the main quad. Not a full week into the start of my first term, and a student – who is my age, as I took a gap year before starting at Oxford – thought there was nothing wrong with coming up to my college room and forcing himself upon me. I should say, it is quite normal for students to spend time in each other's rooms simply to chat or study or drink. These are accepted and friendly activities, but I knew from the moment V and I entered the building in which I was housed that something was not quite right. I thought, can I remember him asking me whether he could come up? I'm sure he must have asked me. Maybe he just wants to talk like all the other students are doing these days.

My inexperience is no excuse for what ensued that evening. He performed not the ultimate act, but a number of related sexual deviances upon me while I grew ever more uncomfortable. I tried to writhe away, but his strength far exceeded my own despite his small frame, and I was unable to move. He then proceeded to spend the night in my room, in my small single bed, in the red and purple sheets I had bought for my new room in college.

I recall every moment of that evening, every sensation, with shame and anger. Every touch, every movement, and every feeling. From the very first week, my whole world was tainted. And so lonesome and friendless was I at the time, that there was nothing I could do about it, and no one I felt comfortable to talk to. He did not want to date me again after the first date, for in his words, I was "too nice" and "too good", which I have since realised nobody should feel regretful of or be shamed for by others.

Unhappily, I could not escape his presence in and around the campus. I was scarred by the memory of that night over and again for the following two years until he graduated and left, as though constantly and spontaneously reliving the trauma every time we were in eyeshot of one another. I will never forget those awkward moments in the dinner hall or the junior common room where our paths would cross and the sickness within me would re-emerge.

My sense of self had been shattered, and during that first year, I often pictured myself as broken. And the broken parts of me were strewn about the college grounds and I alone was brushing together the shards and trying to glue back the pieces of my soul that had been cruelly crushed and discarded.

There were more attempts of this behaviour upon me in the same year from three other male students at my college alone. This came alongside a relationship with a student from a nearby college, who, when I decided to end our relationship as sincerely as possible, frequently texted me under the guise of another student. I later discovered that this other student was in fact a male friend of his, and it was clear to me that he knew all about me. I never again set foot in this nearby college and walked speedily past it with my eyes to the pavement when I had to cross it on my way to lectures.

The sexually-predatorial circles that drew around me at university are not abnormal for a girl in my position. Suddenly, you are away from home and your family, and living in close proximity with students under high pressure who are often looking for a release. Without the constantly watchful eye of parents, families and teachers, these predators have a playground of young, intelligent, physically developed but emotionally growing young ladies at their disposal, living next to them, or across from them, or on a neighbouring quad. All one would need to do as a man is find your way into the room of your victims. Out of absolute fear that word will spread – which it does like wildfire in a closely-confined college – and that you will be shunned for "ratting" out your peers, or that it will tarnish your career prospects, no woman dares ever to speak about it to anyone.

Not only was I mentally traumatised, but I also came down with a severe though unchecked viral chest infection that returned time and again throughout my first year, as my asthma began to develop. As he was coughing frequently throughout our date, I wanted to blame V for this given his treatment of me. Indeed, he made me suffer in many ways and has never and doubtless will ever have to answer for it.

Case 2 | The case of mum in science

I will start this story by describing its end. In the summer of 2020, I discovered from my neurologist that I have mirror movement disorder, an extremely rare condition which presents as involuntarily symmetrical movements of the hands and / or the limbs. Pathologically it has been linked to a mutation in the *Deleted in Colorectal Cancer (DCC)* gene (which we can all agree is a rather worrisome and misleading name), resulting in malformation and misdirection, at the embryological stage, of the axons that innervate the limbs. This could originate either in the cortex or the spinal cord.

After a genetic test (which returned negative for the *DCC* mutation), an MRI scan and a series of electrophysiological studies, it was found that the mirror movements originated in my left motor cortex. The scan showed white matter lesions in the left cortex and are the result of an infarct when I was in my mother's womb. In other words, a loss of oxygen to a part of my developing brain damaged my nerve cells and caused them to develop in a wayward fashion, leading to simultaneous movement of both hands upon movement of just my right hand, and vice versa. The same phenomenon is apparent in my feet also.

As I embark on a long journey with the research team who specialise in this field to determine the true cause of this anomaly and perhaps use this to help others, I am reminded of my mother and an excruciating learning experience I had at the end of my first year at Oxford relating to the condition that ultimately led to her death.

At the time my mother was carrying me, she was only 33 years old (not much older than I am now) and had already had two children and inherited a daughter from my father's first marriage. It was on one fateful day in 1993 – the 26th December to be exact – three years after her third child (me) was born, that she became extremely breathless and was taken to hospital by my father. The team of doctors who examined her dismissed her case, saying she would get better with some rest. She died later that day.

It was unknown at the time, but her third pregnancy with me was very high-risk as she was suffering from a rare autoimmune disease called scleroderma. This was misclassified by her doctors in the year before my conception; and as time went on, the undetected disease took systemic effect, causing her lung tissue to harden and her heart to enlarge and ultimately fail.

I have no memory of my mother at all, save those that I have conjured up in my mind. From the few photos I have seen, and even fewer stories I have heard from my father, I know she was beautiful and kind at heart, not to mention stylish and an extremely good dancer. It is an excruciating realisation that I will never have the pleasure of sharing these gifts with her, or of even hearing her voice or feeling her touch. She has and will always remain the part of me that is empty and missing – the one part that can simply never be replaced.

At the end of my first year at Oxford, after an already harrowing year, I attended a series of Immunology lectures by an esteemed doctor – and one of the kindest of men – who presented evidence that carrying a child could exacerbate pre-existing autoimmune diseases in the pregnant mother. Although stronger evidence was presented to the contrary – that pregnancy can in fact enhance the immune system and dampen the deleterious autoimmune response – I could no longer listen. It had not occurred to me until this moment that perhaps *I* had contributed to the demise of my mother. However weak and vacuous the evidence, that there was even the slightest possibility that this could have been the case tipped me over the edge into the deepest and darkest depression I have ever experienced.

There were but a few weeks before my end of year exams were to commence, and my mind was flooded with darkness. Not only had I had to try and shift this shadow, but I also had to revise the lectures that had caused me so much pain. It felt like torture. No one else knew about it at the time, but as I read through my revision notes, every day up to the day before my first exam, I spent an hour or two quietly though intensely sobbing in my room. No matter how much I tried to motivate myself, I could simply not find any energy. That which I did possess was drained out of me in the form of uncontrollable tears.

I went on to complete my exams but found it hard to genuinely celebrate their end. I went through the motions of smiling and being drenched in champagne and confetti by my friends, but my soul was injured. In the months that followed, I found out that whilst I had passed Neuroscience – which was to become my specialty area – and Physiology, I had failed Biochemistry. I was heartbroken but knew that the emotions that had raged through me in the days leading up to my exams had thwarted my ability to perform. My personal tutor did everything she could to support me, but my Biochemistry tutor simply said, "If you fail again, you have to leave Oxford" without offering much further support. I also spoke to the doctor who gave the lecture – we have remained good friends ever since – who showed me great kindness and support.

Nevertheless, this failure catapulted me into the very depths of my depression. Whilst my peers spent their summers relaxing, or holidaying, I spent them revising again and recovering from a major depressive episode. Moreover, it was the first time I had failed at anything, and I had not the mental capacity or resources to handle it.

And so, the summer was not without its fury. In addition to having to break this news to my father and return to a broken home – as I shall describe later – my depression had taken a new and unfamiliar hold. Two weeks into the summer holiday of revision, I became so low that suicidal ideation became apparent in my thoughts and mind. A strange and dark force within me induced me to, without anyone's knowledge, take the sharpest knife from the kitchen drawer and hide it in the drawer next to my study desk in my room (the haven I mentioned before).

As I revised, my mind would wander to thoughts of the knife. It was the knife we had always used in the kitchen, with a black handle and blade curved over, shaped like the head of an orca. It had been held in my mother's hands once, and my grandfather's (who died the year before and never got to see me go to Oxford), my grandmother's, my uncle's, my father's, my sister's and my brothers', and even in my own hands many times before. Its function was always domestic, to cut the salad or open a parcel. It never served as a weapon of self-destruction, not until that time.

My mind continued to absorb more knowledge through my revision, but it was an extraordinarily draining and uphill battle. They drifted so much to thoughts of the knife that I would occasionally be forced to take it out of the drawer and place it in front on me on the desk just to satisfy the urge.

Every so often, I would run the sharp blade across my wrist, pressing hard enough to leave a white dent or a small scratch, but never enough to physically scar or to kill. I could not go that far; I was too scared. I had to let it out and let the shadows take over for some brief moments, but never to completely destroy me. I had to fight it and I did.

I tried everything imaginable to distract myself when night closed in. I distinctly remember lying in my haven, with just a few streaks of light peeping in from the hallway and listening to a podcast about mindfulness (before mindfulness was quite as prolific as it is today). I remember the sound of the woman's voice on the podcast, deliberately calm and soothing so as to lull one into a sense of profound calm. Yet my legs and arms still twitched with anxiety, as the heaviness in my head deepened and I felt my skull crush into my pillow as if it were a boulder.

It was not until my father confronted me about the missing knife that the game was up. Somebody else knew, so it was no longer my dark secret, my destructive release. In a fit of fury and tears, I returned the knife to him that evening, a week before my re-sit and my half-sister took me upstairs to bed to help me sleep. My father was heartbroken, and despite helping me at the time, hardly ever spoke of it again and did not want anyone else to know. I felt his dismay and disappointment, but also his desire to keep my illness within the confines of the house.

I knew the real reason my sister stayed with me that night was not to help with my insomnia but due the unquestionable fear that she felt of losing her younger sister. It was also perhaps feelings of guilt that had I not been so pressured to be like her throughout my teenage years, things may be different. I might not be so unwell. We did not know it until much later, but this day was to mark the beginning of a long friendship between my half-sister and I, and a sense of togetherness that helped us navigate the rough seas to come.

I passed my exams at the end of the summer and was ready to begin my second year at Oxford. The blip in my academic record disturbs me to this day, but I came out alive. I survived this year however dreadful and traumatic it was. But the year to come was not without its own fresh challenges, and now that the depression had taken hold, I knew deep within that the fight was not over. I knew that no matter how much I cried for my mother she could never return, and thoughts of her passing would forever haunt me. I knew I would be facing this battle with depression for the rest of my life, and I could do nothing but tremble with fear.

Case 3 | The case of C

Some relief was offered in my second year from the fact that I had no exams at the end of this year, and instead needed to complete a term-long research project which would form part of my final grade. This meant Trinity term of my second year could be spent in the Pulmonary Physiology lab at the John Radcliffe Hospital, away from the claustrophobic confines of college. My residence was in college property, but a short distance away from the main college, again offering some respite from the scars of the year just gone.

It was in the lab at the JR that I met a dashing PhD student from Denmark, who I will call C. C was of a shy disposition, and as we sat next to each other in the lab, I often caught him inquisitively glancing over at me as we worked. He would smile at me through his azure blue eyes, and I felt myself blush violently every time we walked by one another in the lab.

In my first month of research, we had many occasions to socialise politely with the whole laboratory. He would invite me to parties at his place in Cowley and I would naturally attend to spend more time with him, in the hopes of gaining his attention and affection. It was clear that this was his motive as well. It was evident that everyone had noticed our attentions to one another, in particular, C's three male colleagues and friends. It was clear to me they had noticed one evening when I invited the team to watch a free concert in my college hall one Sunday, and they encouraged C to sit next to me. Until I listened to it again with my darling G just recently, Brahms' Cello Sonata No. 2 in F major, Op. 99, had never sounded so glorious.

Naturally, they encouraged him to tell me how he felt, and wore him down over the course of the month. One evening, during a team outing to a countryside pub in Oxfordshire, C asked me if I wanted to get some fresh country air with him. It was dark at the time, so we kept near the premises and talked under the soft glow of the lamplights and the brilliance of the moonlight. This is where he confessed his love and admiration for me, and where we had our first kiss. My first true kiss.

I felt all the horrors of the last year melt away with his embrace, and for the first time in what seemed like forever, I felt alive. As the weeks past, and our relationship grew stronger and closer, I began to see our future together. We talked about moving to Copenhagen together after I had graduated and he had finished his PhD, and of my meeting his family there. We even touched on marriage and children in the not-too-distant future. I was grateful that I had found this man who gave me the chance of a future I had no hope of even living through the summer before. I felt so motivated by C and his love for me, that I would study with absolute joy in my heart knowing that when I was done, I could go home to him.

But I will never forget how I was treated at the end. It was in Michaelmas of my third year that a young German girl joined our laboratory. I had been returning to the lab to complete aspects of my research project, and to meet C. This girl was taller and broader than me, and had soft, long, blonde hair, pale blue eyes, and a beautiful complexion. She was perhaps a year older than me, and on an exchange programme from Germany which involved carrying out research in my lab for a term. Her hopes were to become a cancer research scientist, and so naturally, she had a heart of gold.

We became friends and she often commented on C and how lovely we were together. She would attend our dinner parties with the rest of the lab, bringing cupcakes and wine and becoming the centre point of conversation. She even attended my birthday party and gifted me with a stunning blue, black and white zebra striped scarf which I wore religiously over the winter period.

Towards the end of the Michaelmas of my third year in 2012, I noticed C becoming more distant. He would no longer message quite as often or pop over by surprise. He would not want to meet in the café at the JR, saying he was "too busy with work". One day, when my home life was becoming extremely fractured, I asked to talk to him. One Saturday afternoon in November, as we sat upon Headington Hill Park watching the sunset over Oxford, I burst into tears. I explained to him how I was to stay in college over Christmas as the arguments at home were causing me too much pain and disruption. I also asked him why he had been so distant lately.

He held me in his arms, said he loved me, but just after this very moment told me it was over between us. I had not felt so despairing since the summer after my first year and began to weep irrepressibly. He said he had thought about telling me this earlier, but he had to find out from the girl whether he had a chance of a relationship with her instead of me. He told me they had spoken about being together and met several times during the course of our relationship. In essence, he was telling me that he had cheated on me.

I was utterly heartbroken. I felt my world crashing down around me, and every morsel of my body ache and tremble with sadness and fear. I felt intensely alone. He ushered me back to town, and back to my room in college (I was now living in a double room just above the front lodge), where he was to leave me forever.

However, it was not the last I saw of him. He failed to mention it, but he too was staying in Oxford for most of the Christmas holidays. He would not see or console me. I made several attempts to talk to him, if simply to lessen my pain and gain some closure. But he often refused and when he did, was merely a shadow of his former loving self or else made me feel incredibly used. I had no one to turn to for help, and when I finally spoke to a tutor about my problems, she kept me busy with work and around the university campus whilst advising me to "put a pin in it" until my finals were over in the summer.

One day, being alone in college over the Christmas holiday, I fell very sick with a stomach bug and not knowing who else to turn to (my sister was dealing with her own problems which I shall talk about later), phoned C. He came over stricken with worry and armed with food and electrolyte-restoring drinks which he heaped onto the floor by my door. I thanked him but he simply said, "if you need help, you should go and see someone professional". I should mention that he was himself a doctor.

I have since forgiven him for being so cruel and heartless in those last weeks, but it took me many years. I had put my trust in him, I had given him my heart, and he had betrayed me and broken it in every way conceivable.

As with V, he lingered in my life until it was tortuous for me. Even when he had told me he had returned to Denmark permanently the following January (Hilary of my third year), meaning I could return to the research lab without fear of running into him, he had lied. I remember the day as if it were yesterday when I arrived at the lab on the first day of Hilary term, feeling somewhat revived as the new year had begun and could bring fresh opportunities, to find C standing in front of me. He glanced sheepishly at me, knowing he had acted poorly in not telling me that he would still be around the lab, before resuming his work.

Our colleagues in the lab could sense my sorrow and came over to say hello. Even later that morning, C said hello to me, though the guilt was evident in his eyes when he looked at me and in his voice as he spoke. To make the morning worse still, the German girl entered the lab at about 11 though only to collect the last of her belongings from her desk and say a final goodbye to everyone, as she was to return to Germany indefinitely the next day. I felt my heart sink and burn when she said bye and hugged C for the last time – I knew they had had more intimate relations before at my expense, and to see them standing there before me again embracing one another without shame broke me further. I could only think that, despite our beautiful relationship, C had never afforded me the opportunity to say goodbye properly as I deserved. I held in my anger and sorrow and waved the girl goodbye; I never confronted her.

C and I never spoke again which I am grateful for now. Nonetheless, the broken trust would lead me to tumultuous relationships in my 20s and a knack for self-destruction and self-harm that persisted for many years. But eventually, I burnt the love letters C had once given me (which I had kept hidden at the back of my wardrobe) and felt hopeful again for the future.

I have since found true love, with G, who is the most brilliant, kind and generous person I have ever had the great fortune to meet. I know now that C was a waste of my time compared to the magical gift of finding G. Indeed, G has helped me heal, grow and feel truly loved, in the way that everyone deserves to be loved.

Case 4 | The case of my family

My father wanted me to study Economics at Oxford, plain and simple. And, despite gaining a place at Baron to study a subject I love with the hopes of becoming a scientist or doctor one day, my father did not relent at suggesting I switch courses whilst studying. He never failed to mention it every time I saw him (which became increasingly scarce as you may imagine) and the product of this onslaught led to a great anxiety that manifested itself at the end of my first year. On top of an already challenging year – academically and otherwise – I felt at all times like I was "going in the wrong direction" and "should be studying Economics" as my father had wished. I felt like a disappointment to him for not following in his footsteps in business, and even when I did become a management consultant, it was still not good enough.

My frail psyche could barely sustain the pressure and domineering nature of my father, who himself no doubt was and still is contending with a mental health illness. Although, he (and indeed anyone of his generation) would be the last to admit it, let alone get help. And so, my siblings and I were the sounding board for his insecurities and rage.

These notions of disappointment of my chosen path paled in comparison to the hostility he held towards my half-sister. Once an effigy of perfection having graduated in Medicine from Oxford with a triple first-class degree and 8 prizes to her name, a roti-making, pale and beautiful specimen of a Punjabi woman, with charm and kindness as well as skill and intelligence, she was the Indian parents' dream. Her temperament was that of my father's, fiery and passionate, with a tangible aura of self-obsession. I, on the other hand, had to work hard to become nearly as intelligent, and as for beauty, well my eczema held on to it with great force.

But then, my sister did do what any free woman should be allowed to do – fall in love with whomever she wanted to. And this greatly displeased my father. A Belgian neuroscientist, a vegan, who moonlighted as a painter, and still had time to babysit his sister's two children and ride his motorbike (not at the same time thankfully), is not a bad catch at all. He was indeed the perfect match for my sister – they now are married and have a gorgeous son – though my father did not seem to think so.

The intense arguments my father was having with my sister continue in some capacity to this day. However, I experienced the worst of it during my days at Oxford. The arguments at home disrupted my studies to an extraordinary degree.

I remember the day vividly. It was the summer of 2011, when I had just failed my first exam and was sitting beside my father and opposite my sister in Fryer & Bertie's near High Wycombe. I was in sub fusc, feeling exceedingly clownish and looking exceedingly pale.

I could have taken the knife from the pizza plate and ended my pain right there and then. In front of them, in front of everyone. The blood would outpour from my abdomen and stain the pure white shirt that sat beneath my undeserved gown. The colour would depart from my cheeks at an ever-alarming rate, and the last thing I would see before losing consciousness would be the chequered red and green tiled floor of the restaurant.

Perhaps the waitress would smear the garish pink lipstick she had overapplied across her cheek as she held her hand up to gasp in horror. Perhaps her stained palm would sully the phone as she frantically dialled 999. When the paramedics arrive, maybe I am pronounced dead at the scene, and she gets the day off after the shock. She may be thinking, "I am the one who put the knife down beside her, this is my fault. If I had known how she felt, maybe she wouldn't have....".

Of course, none of this did happen. Instead, as I visualised this bloody escape from the reality of my present, my ears were battling the assault of dad and sister. I was merely a victim to them, weak, easily manipulated, "a puppet" as my father would say. They argued about the white European, my now brother-in-law, who supposedly polluted my mind and led to my catastrophic error in failing my exam. It could not possibly be the endless arguing between my dad and sister, between a narcissist and someone ardently defending their position, who cupped my young existence in the palm of their hands and flattened the life out of it. I could not be ill, merely weak and pliable, and someone had to be blamed for this.

I understand why my sister was blind to my feelings; she herself was suffering and dealing with the same conflicting emotions towards my father. Our once beloved father who loved us dearly, when the rest of the world let us all down, had now turned on us. We were at a loss; we had never been prepared for this situation nor did we expect it would ever happen to us. It was not long after that incident that my sister and I realised we needed and wanted to support each other through this turmoil. In a way, we are blessed to have realised this and become the closest of sisters and friends since. As she continued to learn more about my illness, so her compassion and support for me grew. And I came to appreciate the beauty in her passion for life and for helping others, one that was unmatched by anyone until I met G.

With this said, they did not get me the help I desperately needed at the time. I know now that they were afraid of facing their own demons, of finding out whether they too were mentally unwell. My half-sister has come around to the notion of experiencing depressed mood and anxiety from time to time, but my father has never acknowledged his own struggles.

Months and years continued in this vein, and I felt trapped. All the while, I, like Atlas holding the world upon his shoulders, bore the weight of their collective egos until I collapsed. Over time, their voices made me whimper and recoil, like a dog cowering under the sofa on Guy Fawkes night. The very sound would make me wince in pain, and when the amplitude increased, as it always did, I felt like I was dying.

For many years, they continued to argue and blame each other for my failure, rather than considering that I might actually be unwell. It was like being the screwed-up child of divorced parents; but in my case, mother had died, and half-sister had assumed the emotional role but unsuccessfully (she was fighting her own battles) and with the self-serving undercurrents of my father. In fairness, my father tried in his own way to show he cared. I know he loves us dearly, and we love him as our father, but even when we talk about mental health today, is it usually to discuss its potential as a business opportunity.

The rest of the meal was a blur of voices to me. All I can really recall is the distinct feeling that my life was over before it had begun, and that I wanted to die. At the memorial, I thought, they would say I died of severe mental illness or an inability to cope with life. But I would say I died in an unforgiveable accident, crushed and compounded by the weight of two characters until my last breath.

I never did go back to Fryer & Bertie's.

Case 5 | Sugar, wine and samaritans

My ongoing desire to be perfect and to self-destruct was unrelenting into my second and third years at Oxford. In my second year, I began a vicious cycle of excessive running (often causing terrible knee pain), and a diet of cottage cheese, sugar (mainly milk chocolate spread) and red wine. However, my caloric intake did not exceed what I was burning off through over 100km of running each week.

I believe my body was desperately trying to stave off another deep bout of depression in an apparently natural way by constantly exercising (and also thereby not having any time to think about feelings), but the excessive nature of my workouts left me fatigued, faint and unable to sleep well for the entire year.

Insomnia was not a new phenomenon for me. I had faced it in my teenage years and in the summer of the re-sit. Though I recovered from that period, the insomnia persistently returned. I remember suffering from severe insomnia regularly and having to call a Johnny-on-the-spot helpline, and to talk to them endlessly until I fell asleep. I repeated this night after night until I eventually decided to visit my GP who prescribed me diazepam (I was advised by a teacher when I mentioned my problem to just "drink a glass of red wine before bed" instead but this did not seem sensible for someone with depression).

My relationship with C revived me with a vengeance for a time, but when it ended early in my third year, I simply had no reserve left. I was a skeleton of my former self, physically and mentally, and after nearly walking out in front of a bus on St Martin's Street as I emerged from the Dean's office via the back door of college (I spoke to him in a desperate attempt to find meaning in life, but his condescending spiritual and pastoral guidance only made me feel worse), I knew it was time for me to seek professional help.

I remember the GP I saw at the Edward Street Surgery. She was a chirpy middle-aged lady, with a thick, grey boy cut and wearing a bright lilac blouse and pea green corduroys. I will never forget her friendliness and kindness. She was the first in all the medical professionals I encountered to officially diagnose me with MDD and put me on a course of sertraline (a selective serotonin reuptake inhibitor or SSRI), a dose which we titrated over the subsequent six months from 50mg up to 250mg and back down again, from morning to evening until sleep and mood stabilised. Being arguably the most effective pharmacological treatment for depression, unsurprisingly, my depression improved. I was fortunate to not have suffered any side effects apart from the occasional bouts of hypomania and disinhibition at higher doses, which thankfully subsided.

I struggled through my final year, focusing on my academic studies and stabilising on my new medication, undertaking counselling (both individual and group for the first time) whilst maintaining an outward appearance of togetherness. This was Oxford after all, and we are meant to be among the best and brightest, with the glittering personalities and sparkling intellect of leaders. I felt it was vital to maintain my camouflage in order to keep up with my peers as much as possible, though it was exhausting and difficult to maintain as I entered the world of work after university.

Part II. Consulting

"Train people well enough so they can leave,
treat them well enough so they don't want to."
~ Richard Branson

My life as a management consultant, most notably for the first two years when I worked at a large, global corporation, was full of the good, the bad and the ugly of the business world.

My father got his wish; after much bullying (though he will think it persuasion) I was working in business and at a well-established firm. McKennon would always be the gold standard, but one of the big four would do for now, in his eyes.

There is little to say about the content of the work I did there. It was predominantly risk and supply chain consulting, working with life sciences and healthcare organisations alike, and being dispatched to any part of the country (or abroad, such as to Paris, as was the case once, though it was not even remotely glamorous). I started to gain stability in my life in the form of a steady income, allowing me to rent a flat in London, away from the chaos of my home – though home did eventually follow me.

I discovered that being a professional was also a façade for many people at this company, in particular the men. I recall attending an end-of-project team dinner in which a Senior Manager (a married man who had just returned from paternity leave) started talking to a young girl on a dating app and asked her to send him nude photos. She complied, sending photos and videos of herself naked in the shower, in the living room and touching herself. He proceeded to share these photos and videos with the graduate boys and male managers on the team, and even with a couple of ladies (myself included). They were very drunk. I was absolutely horrified by this, but felt that if I left early, it might jeopardise my position on the team. Yet, though I did not show it at the time, that evening I started tactical manoeuvres to get myself out of this company. And once I had achieved this and left the firm, I never spoke to any of them again.

It was not the only occasion where young women were held up as sexual objects to be exploited by powerful, wealthy men. A male friend of mine on the team – a good, diligent young man who had come over from the Netherlands office for the summer – told me our Director had handed him a list of strip clubs he should visit during his time in London.

Along with many cases of abuse I have not the energy to go into, there is one other incident during my time at this firm that was the turning point in my decision to leave. On a long-term project, I served as the central project coordinator, and everyone reported their progress to me, so that I could report this to my Senior Manager, who was a woman. A contractor on the team, who was otherwise a reserve in the army, was hired because of his language abilities. His job was to translate some key documents and report his progress to me. He did so for the first month, increasingly becoming friendly with me. I welcomed his friendship at first, up until it became an infatuation evidenced by a love letter I received from him. I let it go, emphasising our professional and at best, friendly relationship.

But then, he began to comment on my outfits every single day. Sometimes he flattered me and other times he insulted me, but in both cases, I felt uncomfortable. It escalated to such a point that I no longer felt comfortable coming into the office to meet my team, in case I was wearing the "wrong" outfit.

My mentality was to bide my time. He was a contractor after all and was due to finish in a month and then I would not have to see him again if I did not want to. However, one day, after receiving a suggestive comment about my outfit, I told him I was not interested and that I wanted to maintain a professional relationship only. He did not take this outright rejection well and ignored for me for the following two days. It came to a point where he would not talk to me about work progress, and so I was unable to do my job of reporting to senior management. I tried to get him to talk to me and work with me, but unfortunately this was to no avail and I was "blanked" in front of other members of the team time and time again.

Before long, my Senior Manager took me aside and said she had received a complaint about my behaviour. The contractor had told her I was badgering him about work and that he could not focus. I proceeded to give her the full case of harassment I had been experiencing from him, to which she replied: "get used to it". I was aghast. Worse still, she then said: "there are days you may be working late, there will be testosterone flying around, and these things may happen". The tears began to well in my eyes, to which she lastly said: "why don't you take a walk and get yourself sorted out before returning to work".

I fled to the Partner who had hired me, a trustworthy man who immediately dealt with it. The contractor was fired, and the Senior Manager was given a severe warning. Despite this apparently positive reaction, two months after the contractor had left the firm, by which point I had transferred to another department, I heard that the contractor was rehired by the same team to carry on his work.

I am still a management consultant, but thankfully now running my own consulting firm, which is dedicated to making positive changes in the world through supporting mental health services in the UK. But my first job taught me of the harsh realities of the working environment. To this day, I question whether I should have fought more for what is right when I was there. Should I have protected my fellow and future women in the workplace? Would they all turn into this Senior

Manager, become embittered, with stories of harassment of their own?

Undoubtedly so, but I would have been one young woman fighting a global corporation, suffering from depression, and from a broken home. I simply didn't have it in me to fight at this point in my life. But I now wish I had done it. I know I am not alone in thinking this. Many improvements in workplace culture and gender equality have been made since then, but I suspect much of this behaviour still goes on today, to the detriment of many ambitious young women.

Part III. Depression

"...those forlorn regions of dreary space..."
~ Jane Eyre, Charlotte Brontë

I sometimes call my brain The Bad Librarian. For every hand stacking books neatly on a library shelf, the other hand is chucking them out again. This is my mood. Though I am not a librarian, this is very often what I actually do with books, documents, clothes, and anything else I have ordered, in the hope of calming my mind and lifting my mood. I toss things into disarray when the depression takes hold in an attempt to purge myself of dark thoughts.

When suffering from depression, I start to feel alone and sad, because all my memories of happy times and togetherness start to wither, and I lose all concept of myself in relation to the world about me. In other words, I lose perspective, and I am aware of it, only adding to the frustration that accompanies this despondency.

After a while, I do not know where I fit in or whether I belong, because my past experiences become hazy, difficult to recall and without chronology, making it hard for them to inform my present, let alone my future. During the depressive episode, my thoughts become so dark, so hopeless, so bleak, I wonder why I ought to live when all I can give the world and those I love is a black hole of despair and debilitating short-sightedness. If I were a librarian, at this point in my depressive episode, I would throw the books out of the window.

Depression is also inescapable. I liken the feeling to a surfer caught in waves that relentlessly go up and down, in peaks and troughs. Though in this case, sea level is the peak.

With varying severity and at varying times, due to different triggers, I descend to a trough without fail.

As the years have gone by, I have become more familiar with the experience of MDD. I have come to realise that no matter what or how many times I try to counteract its manifestation, it will return, but as happiness is a temporary state, so is this lowness. It will get better. It will pass, if only I ride the wave.

Suffering from MDD feels like a constant state of deterioration and dysfunction. At other times, it feels like my brain is on fire, inflamed and burning with sorrow, such that it withdraws, sinks down, indeed it depresses. I also liken it – as I described to my partner G one day, when I suffered a bad episode – to the feeling of being buried alive.

Whatever the metaphor, feeling depressed and feeling the awful sensations it brings is incredibly challenging. Whilst I have made it dormant again for now, it will awaken and return again. Only age and experience have helped me come to terms with this reality, and I continue to let myself suffer it because of the immense joy one feels when it passes, the temporary but life-giving relief of reaching sea level again.

I | The trough

Despite studying human physiology, after a while, my fascination with life led to a fascination with death. When deep into the realms of major depression, I think so much about death that it becomes a natural part of me. And then, not being able to fear death means I never fully live. I merely exist. I carry out one action after the other. Yet I am not fully aware of myself. Memories are fuzzy and fading, dreams often dark, and sleep fails to refresh.

After the uncontrollable sadness and tears have passed, I become numb, corpse-like, unfeeling of either sadness or happiness or fear or any other emotion. I become an empty vessel, dutifully carrying out my daily activities without feeling or affect, without purpose or consequence beyond keeping me alive. Even then, they are a struggle because, after a long time of losing sight of meaning, without the weight of purpose and emotion, and having been drained of it by the condition, I feel aired out. I feel dry, as if I could crumble under the heel of a small child or float into the sky or drown in the sea and disappear, or injure myself without bleeding, without feeling. When these thoughts set in – what some may call suicidal ideation – I know I am in trouble.

Then, getting out of bed, having a shower, brushing my teeth, getting dressed, even eating are difficult because they require so much energy, energy I cannot muster. No matter how long I lie in bed and dwell on the logic of carrying out these activities, certainly before I can even think about working or exercising or interacting with others, they seem like impossible tasks.

I do not long for attention, for the limelight; in fact, quite the opposite when suffering from depression, I wish I could disappear altogether. I feel I am an outsider, looking in, watching others go about their lives, never quite being able to be a part of it. I never quite feel strong or confident enough, so frightened I am by the words of others, so low is the opinion I have of myself and my worth, and so desperate I become to hide it and pretend everything is fine.

I have really come to dislike the word "fine" and never use it anymore in response to the question "How are you?". Few people who say they are fine are truly fine. They are often crying out for help, something my partner G very astutely catches me out on. Thankfully, I fall less frequently and less deeply into the trough these days, in large part thanks to my loving and patient G. He is my world and everything in it. My love, my lifeboat, my joy, my reason for living. And I am eternally grateful to the forces that be for finding him and finding love, just when I was about to give up hope.

II | The peaks / sea level

Having reached the deepest trough of my depression at the age of 20, I felt like an overly ambitious scuba diver recovering from the bends, determined to ensure this dangerous depth was never reached again, and to keep within safe limits. I knew, somehow intuitively though, as would be confirmed by my doctor, that I would suffer from depression again. What I could control however was how badly the recurrence was felt, how bad the bad would be and how good the good would be.

The peaks were and continue to be worth the enormous struggle. When I say peaks, as I say, I mean baseline, I mean sea level – not the mania and hypomania experienced in bipolar disorder – but the "normal" level of joy, or the stable, sound mood if you prefer. These happier times have indeed been full of joy, time with my love G, holidays, time spent with family and friends, watching movies, eating incredible food, dancing. But the truly best experiences came when everyday tasks that seemed insurmountable during the depressive period became easy, even pleasant and enjoyable. Tasks like cooking, dressing nicely for the day, even eating.

One of my greatest comforts and pleasures to this day is having a cup of tea in the morning. It signals to me that I have slept, I have taken care of my body, I am awake, I am alive, I have made it out of bed, I have made it to the kitchen, I am nourishing and awakening my mind and body, my gastrointestinal system is switching on, and there is a whole day ahead of me full of possibilities. It is amazing to think that a mug with nothing but boiling water, milk and a tea bag carry so much meaning and purpose. Admittedly, it would be even better with a raisin scone, jam and clotted cream, in bed, reading, with my darling next to me. But unfortunately not every day is a Saturday.

I know dear reader you will have heard many times that there is incredible joy and purpose in small things. I would not have thought it 10 years ago when I was first diagnosed with MDD, nor in the years that proceeded as I adjusted (or occasionally maladjusted) to taking sertraline or when I pushed myself hard physically and mentally to achieve constantly and often became very depressed.

Living with depression – and indeed any other mental health condition – means going on a journey. Indeed, it involves experiencing scary and difficult emotions, receiving a diagnosis that labels you and may even make you vulnerable to stigma and abuse, taking medications that cause side effects or changes in mood you have not experienced before, and maybe losing friends because you need that time to care for yourself or because they no longer know how to treat you.

The journey of recovery I believe really began the day I said to myself, "I want to get better". From that moment, with the right people around me, on the right medication, with a brilliant therapist, I began to make life decisions with my health in mind and this has made all the difference.

I never ever want to feel like I did that day I nearly walked out in front of a bus, or cut myself with a knife, or the day I sobbed under my desk for hours at Oxford, or the day I failed my exam. But to get better, I know I must remember in the here and now that I have the power to fight my feelings of shame, guilt, loss and loneliness. With that, I found purpose in life, I found love, I started to enjoy the things that felt good not made me sound good, and I realised that my hardships could be strengths to help others.

I found purpose in my life through wanting to get better. But there is nothing special about me, anyone is capable of this. I believe in me and I believe in you, which is why we should never stop fighting for the feeling of being alive.

Part IV. Childhood

"Because I feel that, in the Heavens above,
The angels, whispering to one another,
Can find, among their burning terms of love,
None so devotional as that of "Mother" "
~ To My Mother, Edgar Allan Poe

I | Mother

Since losing my mother at the of 3, I have never felt quite complete. For me growing up, having a fantasy life with a mother was better than accepting the reality of her death. I went from having the fantasy of a mother to the fantasy of the perfect mind, the perfect job, the perfect family, the perfect relationship. Indeed, since I finally came to accept the loss of my mother in recent years, facilitated by my wonderful therapist, my quest for perfection has equally diminished. I am much better off without it.

In previous years, a sort of mystery surrounded my mother which was augmented by a recurring dream I had time and again over a period of nearly 15 years. I often wonder whether this dream is actually my earliest and perhaps only memory of my mother, or whether it is a by-product of losing her at such a young age. As you will see, I suspect it is a combination of both: fragments of dreams and reality blended together as in a painting, but where the middle is grey. As if both ends of that painting were trying to run away from each other, as if they were so different, so opposite, that the place in which they ought to overlap is empty.

As I describe the dream now, I am pleased to say that I no longer experience it. Thanks to the happiness I have found in my life and the hours spent psychologically unravelling my feelings towards my mother with my therapist, my brain has at last let it go. But nonetheless, here it is:

Picture a small girl of no more than 3 or 4 years of age, with fine long brown hair, small sparkling brown eyes, golden skin, and chubby cheeks. She is wearing a blue satin dress, her absolute favourite dress, which reaches down to her small, knobbly knees; a dress with puffy shoulders and small white pearls embellishing the torso. The shine of her dress against the warm lighting made her feel special.

On her feet are little white ankle socks, frilly at the upper edges. She is wearing a pair of shiny black shoes – those that young girls wear in the early years of school – with a small belt buckle halfway up with a vertical black strap down the middle, leaving two empty sections, shaped like church windows, through which the white socks appear. She wears a pale pink bow in her hair, one that in later years, her grandmother used to pin in her long locks before school.

This little girl is very energetic and so full of life, love and laughter. She is standing in the living room of what is the first house she recalls, in Leeds. The house is modest, but to her, the lengthy living room is very grand. She knows it is her grandparent's house.

At the opening of this dream, this young girl skips towards her mother, who is perched on the edge of a cushy light brown sofa, ready to receive her daughter in her outstretched arms. The mother is very beautiful, with a beaming smile, golden brown skin, and equally fine and undulated light brown hair. She is wearing a pale blue and pale green Indian dress, with a beige cardigan over her shoulder, and round gold earrings in which pearls delicately rest in the centre. Her eyes are bright and lively, and her lips painted red. She is stylish and yet full of warmth and tenderness.

The little girl frolics over to her mother, hugs her tightly, and twirls around in her blue frock. The girl stops as she notices the bow on the back of her dress has become loose, its two tethers hanging free at either side of her. With her hands sweetly poised together in front of her, she asks her mother to help her retie the bow. Her mother, smiling even more brightly, ties the little girl's bow, and the little girl skips merrily off.

This girl skips right across the length of the living room, past another set of single sofas. But as she does so, the lights begin to dim around her. There is a chill in the air, a growing crispness and an eerie darkness. It is grey here. The little girl continues to skip to the far end of the room, a bit more cautiously now, where at one side there is a solid oak dining table that her grandfather built, covered in a scarlet cloth. The gloomy sky overlooks her through the doors to the garden.

The room slowly fades into a dark grey. No light dares to wander here, she thought. She notices this half of the room is full of family – people she senses she has seen before, though no one, save her father, grandparents, brothers and sister she cares to notice. She can't really make out their faces in any case, they are blurry to her.

Her blue satin dress is still bright amongst the gloom. She ventures further through the crowd of people and sits in her father's lap. Her father is looking at something in the centre of the crowd and tears are flowing down her father's face and she notices her grandparents and siblings are also weeping. She traces their eyes to the centre of the room to see a coffin, and in this coffin, lies the little girl's mother.

Inside, it feels now as if she has been pierced somewhere where her heart lies, and the pain, that unbearable pain, radiates throughout her entire body, paralysing her muscles, and slowly draining her life and energy. So unbearable is this pain, the only option is to bury it. Bury it deep inside, and never let it get out.

As the little girl digs deep within her to bury this pain, a hole emerges right through her. As the hole becomes apparent, she starts to feel numb throughout her body. Desperately, she tries to refill the hole with the broken pieces of herself she had tossed asunder, but nothing could fill it. As the party disperses and the coffin disappears, the girl realises days have gone by and the hole has become jagged and rotten. The pale blue satin dress is now grey and scratched at the elbows.

Every time I have this dream, I wake up suddenly at this point, my skin is drenched in sweat and I am breathing heavily. As I begin to reflect on the dream, despite having had it many times before, I naturally begin to think about my mother. As I have aged, I have gone from feeling sad and despairing when I wake up, to feeling grateful for having experienced my mother's love and affection, even if it was only in a dream.

The best way I can sum up what I know of her character is that, as my father once told me, when on her death bed at the age of 33, my mother's last words were "who will take care of my darling children?".

Of all the traumas I have described, losing my mother was the deepest and most jagged of them all. But Einstein was right, that imagination is our most important asset. By imaging my life with her in it, what she would have thought and done in the situations I encounter, what she would have thought about the people I meet, how she would embrace and enjoy sewing and dancing and cooking as I do, she is always with me.

II | Uncle

It was a jagged time. At the age of 12, I was powerless to help him. Now, at 30 years of age as I read about intellectual disabilities, I feel an intense sense of despair and sorrow. It was a life wasted – a good man's life – that of my uncle F.

I will never forget the day we visited uncle F at the care home for adults with intellectual disabilities, a sullen, decaying, beige building which resembled more a prison than a care home. Yet I remember, despite its appearance, that it housed some of best and kindest of people: the care workers.

My other uncle was visiting then. He was a wealthy doctor from New York, the eldest of the five brothers that included my father (though they all followed a line of three older sisters). I will always remember that he did nothing to help uncle F. His courtesy visits to the care home were merely that, a box-ticking exercise.

My siblings and I were not taken inside much to see my uncle F, as my father and grandparents thought it would be too distressing. One day when I was 12, we visited but I stayed in the car with my siblings. When my father and grandparents emerged from the home with the rich uncle (on one of his courtesy visits from the States), my father broke down in tears. By instinct and having grown up with uncle F and come to love him, I began to cry too, as did my brothers, half-sister and grandparents. But the rich uncle just stood at the car door beside my father, not a wet gleam in his eye, and simply patted my father's back. It will be OK, he said. It's best for him, he said.

My uncle F lived with my grandparents in Leeds, and when my mother died, we moved in with them. From a young age, I remember watching my uncle and wondering what had happened to him. He was overweight, his hair unkempt though mostly hidden under a navy-blue turban with only an uneven beard and moustache visible, and his left eye was focused outward. I remember his clothes; he always wore classic blue denim jeans, a pale blue shirt under a brown woollen sweater, and slip-in adidas black and white sandals. I wish I had his clothes now as a memory of him.

Uncle F loved his parents dearly, and they too loved and cared for him. He was certainly not malicious. Indeed, it was not his fault that he was this way. I had a sense even as a young girl that despite his learning difficulties, he had a kind heart. I would never call him "Molly" as my siblings did, I could not be so derogatory or mimic the cruelties of others. I thank my sensitive soul I never treated him ill and only had thoughts of caring for him and speaking to him, if only I had the maturity, courage and faculties for it at the time. I admit as a young girl, I was afraid of his large stature and of saying the wrong things. But most of all, I was afraid of my father.

My father loved his brother and cared for him, but his own limited personality traits and profound sense of despair after losing his wife often threw him into fits of extraordinary anger. When uncle F would do something wrong, even speak or walk into the room at the wrong time, my father would shout at him and sometimes even slap him. His voice would become so loud, it deafened my ears, as it did in later years, and I would hide behind the sofa or under the kitchen counter until the violence passed. My grandfather – old, sweet and passive – could not stand up to the domineering figure of my dad.

Uncle F would retreat into his room upstairs, the look of absolute terror sheathed only by a single tear in his eyes, on a face reddened by slaps and shame. This is a picture still so vivid in my mind, that as I write this it evokes tears. I can learn to understand but not entirely forgive my father for his treatment of F. After all, he did not know how to treat him either and this was all he was capable of doing. I try to empathise with my father, even though my heart still aches with pity and sorrow for my uncle.

Despite this, of all the disparate clan, my father and grandparents were the only people who really loved and cared for uncle F. For most of my life and his life, he lived at home with family (including my loving mother), with parents, his brother and children around him. When he moved to a care home, the workers were kind and often took him and others at the home on trips to the farm and on country walks. They were kind (at least, I certainly want to think and believe this was always the case) and I am grateful to them for this.

As for uncle F's other siblings, I will never forget their negligence. Throughout my childhood, whilst they were holidaying in Europe and the Caribbean, or throwing lavish parties with friends and other family members (not us) in London, uncle F was in a care home in Cross Green without family, probably confused, and certainly frightened. And my father, my siblings and I were struggling at home without mother, with dying grandparents and with an uncle in care we constantly worried about though struggling too much ourselves to help him. I try to understand the extended family, to empathise with them, and to be outwardly kind as I believe everyone should be treated kindly. But still I cannot forget their negligence, and I sometimes wish I felt strong enough to hold them all accountable for their selfishness and neglect.

The four of us all suffered trauma and mental health problems without knowing it (my half-sister suffered anxiety, one of my brothers OCD and my father, a personality disorder and depression). They are all undiagnosed and still very much in denial, unlike me and my MDD. We rarely had friends over because we could barely feed ourselves, let alone guests, and worried about exposing them to uncle F before we sent him to the home (I often despise myself for even thinking this. Why should F's disability have mattered so much? Why did we feel shame?).

A few years later, just shortly before I received a place to study at Oxford, my dear grandfather died in our arms at Leeds General Infirmary. He suffered from congestive heart failure and at the age of 95, suffered an aspiration and his heart gave way within 3 hours. I still remember the look in his eyes when he walked into the kitchen after aspirating as the colour faded from his face before me. Just 3 months later, my grandmother died from a series of strokes caused by metastasised pancreatic cancer, and 6 months after this, my dear uncle F contracted severe pneumonia at the care home one winter. After several days on a ventilator (again at Leeds Hospital) he also died with us in the room beside him.

I was always too frightened to tell uncle F how much we loved him, how much I loved him. I was a terrified little girl without a voice, and there was nothing I could do. I have to remember this and forgive myself. But if uncle F was here today, I would say the world and your family failed you, but you are and were always loved and that you did nothing to deserve your fate. If I had the ability at the time, I would have helped you.

Though this is not possible now, I am thankful that our lives crossed, if but briefly. Uncle F taught me perhaps the most important lesson of my life: to be kind and sensitive to the needs of others. This was always a part of my character, but with maturity and upon reflection of my time with him, I no longer feel weak or ashamed for having this attribute. Kindness is and always will be a strength.

As an aunty myself now, I better understand what you hope for from the children who enter your life: love, consideration, communication, perhaps just a hug from time to time. Instead I bore my father's burden, absorbed his fears, and did not give uncle F the attention he deserved, the sort that does not care if your eyes are a bit funny, or your speech is a bit slow and slurred. The sort that looks for laughter and joy even in the face of sadness.

But, in the end then, dear uncle F's life has not been wasted. I will hold him in my heart, until I can help others as he should have been helped and until I can bring joy to others as joy should have been brought to him.

Part V. Self-Discovery

"...yes, in spite of all,
Some shape of beauty moves away the pall
From our dark spirits."
~ John Keats, Endymion (Book I)

A wise woman once told me that I have a superpower, and that my superpower is kindness. Like Chiron the wounded healer, I am now compelled to use my lived experiences of depression to help others who suffer from mental health illness. I hope in doing so, I do not inflict or even project my pain on others, but use it as a wise teacher, a guide, or a trusted advisor to navigate the complex pathways of other psyches in an attempt to heal and soothe.

As I say, riding the wave of depression occurs in peaks and troughs, and over the years, I have come to accept this reality. Depending on the day, the time of month, my general health and sometimes on nothing particular at all, I will descend into a trough. In these times, I quite often picture myself at the bottom of a whirlpool looking up at a grey stormy sky and wondering how I am going to get out (a bit like Ariel at the end of The Little Mermaid, staring up helplessly at the evil Ursula).

Though experience and love have been my saving graces over time (for which I am forever grateful, especially in the current pandemic), throughout lockdown, I have nonetheless been fighting the tides that run against me.

Perhaps I am not alone in thinking this in the era in which we live. Am I anxious or depressed or both? In truth, I have experienced every emotion in the last year, since lockdown began.

What if I get COVID-19 and die from going grocery shopping? What if I make my partner or my family sick with COVID-19? I have tried to deal with this anxiety and accompanying low mood by typing out some of my fears in as many fonts as I had the energy to create:

What if I get COVID-19?
What if I get COVID-19?
WHAT IF I GET COVID-19?
What if I get COVID-19?
What if I get COVID-19?
What if I get COVID–19?
What if I get COVID–19?
What if I get COVID-19?
What if I get Covid-19?
What if I get COVID-19?
What if I get COVID-19?
What if I get COVID-19?

By making these anxieties appear is different forms, I somehow diminish their value.

Writing became a hobby and release for me when I was a child, though I had also turned to other art forms, particularly drawing and painting. These extracts of my mind and heart were scribbled upon every form of nearby material – a scrap of newspaper, the nearest napkin, the margin of my schoolbooks – as and when the words came to me and when the feelings pressed against my skin, desiring to leap out and immortalise themselves upon the page.

Recurring shoulder and knee pain are my proverbial canaries in the mine in terms of signalling my decline into depression. Nevertheless, I have found that as soon as I start engaging in one of my hobbies, which often involve being creative or being active, these psychosomatic symptoms disappear. I begin to feel myself again. Some of my favourite and most effective, creative, de-stressing and elevating activities include ballet, sewing, painting, baking, yoga, watching a movie, and even doing the housework. Sharing my life with G and spending time with loved ones when it is possible is without question joyful as well. I force myself to remember why I love these activities, hoping and at times succeeding to fall in love with them all over again. I certainly fall in love with G over and again every day we wake up next to each other. I have the great privilege of gazing into his beautiful blue-green (with a dash of brown) eyes before I even know what hour of the morning it is. Over time, I have come to realise and accept that there is no need to stop doing what I love and enjoy, even if I will not be the expert at it. The journey is what makes it worth it.

I was recently asked to say what my "compassionate colour" is and without hesitation, I said yellow. For whatever reason, each of the following items came into my mind when I thought of yellow, and in this rather random order. Yellow is the colour of:

- A summer's day
- Fires, candles, light bulbs
- Wheat fields and mustard fields
- Yellow roses, daffodils, the centre of daisies, sunflower petals, yellow tulips, marigolds
- Bumblebees and wasps (at least half of them)
- Chicks
- Trees near Rogie Falls in Scotland (G and I visited in August)
- The stone in Oxford, Cambridge, Bath
- Food – scones, butter, bananas, lemons, white wine (sort of), light beer, camomile tea, egg yolk, scrambled eggs, potatoes, pancakes, custard, cheese
- Some leaves in the autumn
- Space, Venus, the stars, the moon, the rings of Saturn (I think)

- Sand, tropical fishes
- Tennis balls
- Emojis, whether happy, sad, in love, angry, sick, hungry
- Minions, Belle's dress, The Simpsons
- Klimt, van Gogh, Monet, da Vinci
- The Colosseum, the Golden Temple, the Pyramids, the Brandenburg Gate, the trams in Lisbon, and the taxis in New York

Everything I thought of was positive and happy and made me feel good in some way. I surprised myself with how many associations I made. I realised then that yellow is the colour that makes me happy and smile, and no surprise then that it is my compassionate colour. It makes me feel warm and nurtured, and it makes me more compassionate towards others.

Something as simple as changing the light bulb in the lamp on my desk to a warm yellow hue has had an immediate and cumulative effect of making me feel happier, more focused, more empathetic, more awake and alive. I have always had this connection to the colour (I had a similar lamp on my desk in the room I once called my haven in adolescence). With time, I have appreciated the impact this has had and can still have on my mental health.

I never thought that such a simple question could yield such a deep understanding of my psyche. Perhaps other colours represent other emotions – anger, fear, sadness, disgust – though this is not a new concept when you have watched Inside Out. These days, I try to sit on my feelings, to hold them without letting them take over. I like to know they are there. They are a sign that I exist, and that I am human, which means I am adaptable and intelligent, but also feeling.

The same wise women told me "the breath comes first". I am hopeless at meditation, but I enjoy yoga which (especially for someone with asthma like me) is an excellent way of connecting with the breath. There is something about connecting with audible breath whilst stretching that generates a deep sense of calm, and by the end, as I lie in Savasana, I am enveloped in a beautifully still but incredibly loud silence.

This sounds odd to me still, and even silly on days when I cannot seem to "connect with the breath" at all! But I remind myself that I am here doing an activity that is beneficial to the mind and body, that I am breathing and that I will not always be able to breathe, let alone connect mindfully to this breathing. I remind myself that when I can and do connect to it, it is an asset and a means of grounding, soothing and relaxing myself. For these reasons, it is worth the time.

With this practice, which also involves forgiving myself for times I fail to connect with my breath or do a yoga move deeply, I have learnt that the breath must always come first. The breath is life-giving but is also a constant that we cannot live without. By holding such an important place in existence, it comes at the centre of all I do. I appreciate it for its vital purpose, as the breath is not only calming and nourishing, but essential.

By making the breath the first thing I think about before I think about anything else, I re-invite into my body and mind a feeling of calm, collectedness, life and vitality unequal to any other sensation. It is a way of being kind to myself, so that I can proceed with the day or task at hand calmly, mindfully, as myself and with my own thoughts unclouded by others or by the demon of depression. It reminds me of the importance of being healthy and caring for myself, no matter what the day brings.

My last words to you are, as one of my best friends would say to me when I was in low spirits: "Head down, chin up. You are stronger than you think. Never give up".

Afterword

Thank you for sharing this journey with me. Many people have called me brave for writing this book and talking openly about my condition. But if just one person can be helped by its content, then it is worth everything.

I am grateful to say that after living with major depression for over ten years now – as far as I know – I have come to accept its presence. Over time, it has become less intrusive in my life. With the experiences I have had, and people I have met on the way, I am more confident that I can avoid such near-fatal episodes as I have suffered in the past.

Through this process, I have come to appreciate the people in my life so much more: my extraordinary therapist who gave me the inspiration for this book and its central metaphor; my immediate family who have raised me, helped me and loved me in the ways they know how to; my friends young and old who have accepted my openness, shared their own stories, and not left my side; and the love of my life, G, who is the most affectionate, patient and supportive person I have ever had the good fortune to meet, to love and to be loved by. I am grateful to have my wonderful nephew S too who has taught me what childhood joy should look like and who has brought so much happiness to our lives without really knowing it (yet).

Some of these relationships, as you have read, were not without their many bumps and bruises. Some are long gone, some fleeting, some never took off fully, and others have been on the verge of total collapse at points in the past. Yet others have been a joy from day 1. In any case, I feel better waking up each day knowing that if something feels wrong, I will not suffer it alone. These people all know who they are, and when they read this, I hope they know that I am eternally thankful and that I love them.

I have left behind the vision of perfection, and these days, in my spare time, I focus on embracing the new, the creative and the invigorating. This has varied from oil painting for the first time, learning how to sew cushion covers and cross stitch personalised bookmarks, baking scones, cakes and casseroles, to cycling the North Coast 500 route in Scotland on a tandem with G, climbing Mount Washington, and taking ballet lessons every week for the last two years. I try not to forget other self-care techniques in all of this: doing yoga, taking a hot bath and listening to a fun podcast (ideally without dropping my phone in the tub!), painting my nails, going for a walk and breathing in fresh air, or simply sitting and breathing. When I do work, it is to learn more about my condition and other mental health conditions and services, and to try and help and encourage others.

There are days when the depression creeps back, seemingly for no reason, causing a few nights of insomnia and low mood. But, with G's help, I am reminded of my arsenal of self-help techniques to stop sinking further into it. They don't and won't always work, but that's OK. I try again until something does work, and this may mean doing nothing at all, which is OK too. I try to remember that looking after myself is the most important and kindest thing I can do. It benefits me and those around me.

But there is no longer any pressure to be the best me all the time. Every day, I listen to my mind and my body and ask them one question: "How are you feeling today?".

~ K

Lightning Source UK Ltd.
Milton Keynes UK
UKHW041547310521
384682UK00001B/230

9 781914 195259